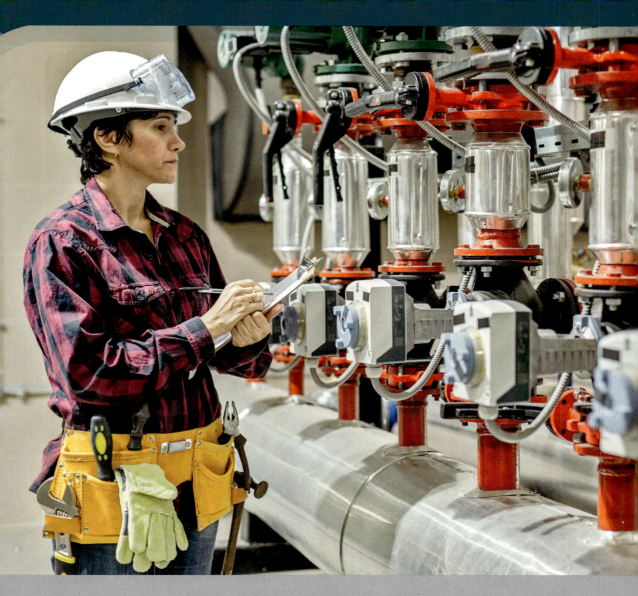

WORKING IN
ENGINEERING

by Vicki C. Hayes

12 STORY LIBRARY

www.12StoryLibrary.com

12-Story Library is an imprint of Bookstaves and Press Room Editions

Produced for 12-Story Library by Red Line Editorial

Photographs ©: nimis69/iStockphoto, cover, 1; Rawpixel/iStockphoto, 4; shironosov/iStockphoto, 5; AlexRaths/iStockphoto, 6; Roger Dale Pleis/Shutterstock Images, 7; powerofforever/iStockphoto, 8; anandaBGD/iStockphoto, 9; nd3000/iStockphoto, 10; Triff/Shutterstock Images, 11; golubovy/iStockphoto, 12; Hannes Grobe CC 3.0/Wikimedia Commons, 13; Jirat Teparaksa/Shutterstock Images, 14; AuntSpray/Shutterstock Images, 15; miker/Shutterstock Images, 16; Aneese/iStockphoto, 17; Jeremy Thompson CC 2.0, 18; monkeybusinessimages/iStockphoto, 19, 28; Petty Officer 3rd Class Patrick Kelley/U.S. Coast Guard Atlantic Area, 20; endopack/iStockphoto, 21; torwai/iStockphoto, 22; VladCa/iStockphoto, 23; Dmitry Kalinovsky/Shutterstock Images, 24; johnrandallalves/iStockphoto, 25; Elena Muzykova/Shutterstock Images, 26; Nuclear Regulatory Committee, 27, 29

Library of Congress Cataloging-in-Publication Data

Names: Hayes, Vicki C., author.
Title: Working in engineering / by Vicki C. Hayes.
Description: Mankato, MN : 12 Story Library, 2017. | Series: Career files | Includes bibliographical references and index. | Audience: Grades 4 to 6.
Identifiers: LCCN 2016047454 (print) | LCCN 2016048183 (ebook) | ISBN 9781632354440 (hardcover : alk. paper) | ISBN 9781632355119 (pbk. : alk. paper) | ISBN 9781621435631 (hosted e-book)
Subjects: LCSH: Engineering--Vocational guidance--Juvenile literature.
Classification: LCC TA157 .H417 2017 (print) | LCC TA157 (ebook) | DDC 620.0023--dc23
LC record available at https://lccn.loc.gov/2016047454

Printed in the United States of America
022017

Access free, up-to-date content on this topic plus a full digital version of this book. Scan the QR code on page 31 or use your school's login at 12StoryLibrary.com.

Table of Contents

Who Can Be an Engineer? 4

Biomedical Engineers Lend a Helping Hand 6

Civil Engineers Make Structures Safe 8

Robotics Engineers Design Amazing Machines 10

Computer Hardware Engineers Keep Going Smaller 12

Aerospace Engineers Take to the Skies 14

Forensic Engineers Figure Out Failures 16

Mechanical Engineers Keep Machines Running Smoothly . 18

Environmental Engineers Protect the Planet 20

Marine Engineers Explore New Depths 22

Electrical Engineers Develop New Ways to Use Power 24

Chemical Engineers Search for the Right Formulas 26

Other Jobs to Consider 28

Glossary 30

For More Information 31

Index 32

About the Author 32

Who Can Be an Engineer?

What does an engineer do? Engineers are people who make things work. They use their imagination to invent, design, and build. Things such as the Mars rover, the Hoover Dam, and the first solar panels were all built by engineers.

There are dozens of types of engineers. They work in hundreds of different areas.

Most engineers use math every day. For example, civil engineers use math to figure out how many vehicles can drive on a bridge at one time. Many engineers also use science. Food companies work with chemical engineers. These engineers mix different chemicals to mimic the taste of certain foods.

Engineers are often hired to solve problems.

Engineers work together to find solutions.

Engineers can work in many different environments.

They have to be creative to come up with solutions. Sometimes they work with teams. Other times, they work on their own. Engineers must be organized. They also have to be good at noticing little details. These details are often the key to solving big problems.

2 million
Estimated number of engineers working in the United States.

- Engineers love to invent, explore, build, and imagine.
- There are many different types of engineers.
- Many engineers use both math and science in their jobs every day.
- Engineers are good problem solvers.

MAKERSPACES

Makerspaces are places where people go to create, invent, and build things. The spaces help users explore different materials, such as plastic, wood, and cardboard. In the spaces, users can experiment to try to solve problems. Many makerspaces are for kids. They can often be found at local libraries and museums.

Biomedical Engineers Lend a Helping Hand

Biomedical engineers work in medicine. They work in hospitals, laboratories, and university research departments. They design tools to help doctors better understand patients' health. Sometimes these tools are machines. For example, biomedical engineers are working to create better imaging machines to see inside the body. These machines could create clearer scans of the brain. That would help doctors learn more about how certain brain diseases work.

Sometimes the tools biomedical engineers design are used by patients themselves. People with bad hip joints and knee joints need new ones. Biomedical engineers continue to design new artificial joints. They try to make the joints move as naturally as possible. Biomedical engineers also design artificial arms and legs. These are called prosthetics.

Biomedical engineers work to improve medicine.

$86,220

Average salary for biomedical engineers in the United States in 2015.

- Biomedical engineers work in universities, hospitals, and laboratories.
- They design tools to help doctors treat patients.
- Some biomedical engineers make artificial hip joints, knee joints, and limbs.
- Biomedical engineers need to have good communication skills and usually need to earn a bachelor's degree.

INTERNSHIPS

An internship is a great way to get a feel for what an engineer does. Interns can learn a lot about a particular field in just a few weeks. Most internships are for college students. They usually occur in the summer. Generally, internships involve on-the-job training. Sometimes interns get paid. Sometimes they do not. But the experience can help with getting a good job later on.

Biomedical engineers need to have good communication skills. They have to write reports about their research. They sometimes have to explain the results of their experiments to people who are not experts. Biomedical engineers usually need a bachelor's degree. Coursework for a biomedical engineering degree includes many classes in biology.

Biomedical engineers design prosthetic legs.

7

Civil Engineers Make Structures Safe

The Hoover Dam stands on the border between Arizona and Nevada. It is more than 726 feet (221 m) tall. The dam is made of concrete. The concrete in the dam is a precise mixture of gravel, sand, and other materials. Getting the concrete mixture just right is the work of a civil engineer.

Civil engineers design and plan many big things. Highways, bridges, railways, and water systems are all built with the help of civil engineers. Some civil engineers work for the government. These engineers help plan a city's road repairs and construction. They make sure sidewalks are easy for people with disabilities to use. Other civil engineers work for private companies. They help figure out how to fit the most parking stalls into a store's lot. They make sure

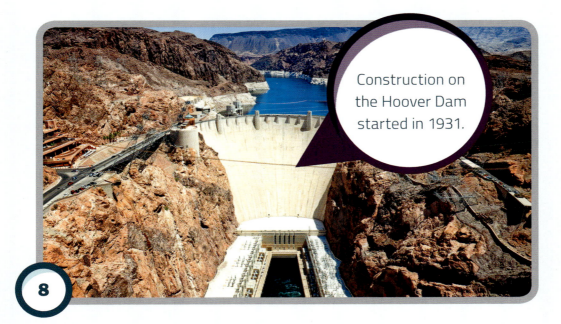

Construction on the Hoover Dam started in 1931.

Engineering technicians often perform inspections by surveying.

dirt is sloped away from a building's exterior to discourage flooding.

Civil engineers usually need a bachelor's degree. Many states also require civil engineers to pass a test before becoming licensed to approve construction plans. Civil engineers often work closely with civil engineering technicians. Technicians help engineers collect data. Sometimes they also help inspect construction. Most civil engineering technicians earn an associate's degree.

4 million

Estimated number of miles (6.4 million km) of public roads in the United States.

- Civil engineers design and plan big things, such as highways and bridges.
- Some civil engineers work for the government, while others work for private companies.
- Most civil engineers need a bachelor's degree and have to pass a state license test.
- Civil engineering technicians need an associate's degree.

THINK ABOUT IT

City engineers have to listen to concerns from citizens, who may not agree with their design plans. Should city engineers delay needed construction if the plans are unpopular? Why or why not?

Robotics Engineers Design Amazing Machines

There are many different kinds of robots. Some are robotic machines. They can do certain jobs faster than humans can. Robotic machines can do dangerous jobs so humans will not get injured. Some robots can do work where people cannot easily go, such as outer space or the deep sea. All these robots have one thing in common. They were designed by robotics engineers.

Many robotics engineers work with manufacturers. The engineers design robotic arms to make production processes move faster.

Other robotics engineers create mobile robots. Since the 1970s, the US military has used robots to defuse bombs. A human can control the robot from a safe distance. In 2003, the National Aeronautics and Space Administration (NASA) launched the Mars rover *Opportunity*

Robotics engineers often work as part of teams to develop robots.

CURIOSITY

In 2011, NASA engineers launched a new Mars rover called *Curiosity*. This robot gathers data to help scientists figure out if Mars could have ever supported life. Robotics engineers equipped *Curiosity* with camera eyes and a robot arm. *Curiosity* is not the only robot traveling around on Mars, though. *Opportunity* is still working and sending data back to Earth.

into space. Engineers on Earth used computers to send commands to the rover. The rover's antennas picked up the instructions. *Opportunity* landed on Mars and followed the commands to collect data for NASA scientists.

Robotics engineers need to earn a bachelor's degree. To get ahead in the field, some robotics engineers choose to earn advanced degrees, too. All robotics engineers must be creative. They have to think of ways new technology can make robots even better.

1804
Year Joseph-Marie Jacquard programmed a machine to follow a set of instructions from paper cards.

- Robotics engineers work with machines.
- Robots are designed to do jobs that human cannot easily do.
- Many robotics engineers design robots to cut down on manufacturing time, and others create mobile robots.
- Robotics engineers need to earn bachelor's degrees, and some earn advanced degrees.

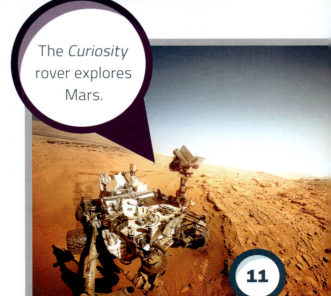

The *Curiosity* rover explores Mars.

Computer Hardware Engineers Keep Going Smaller

Each computer is made up of many different parts. There are circuit boards, processors, and memory devices, just to name a few. All of these pieces must work together. Computer hardware engineers make sure that they do.

Many computer hardware engineers are working to make computers smaller. Some computers in the 1960s were as big as entire rooms.

These engineers are also working to make computers lighter. The first laptops designed in the 1980s were four to five times heavier than the laptops of today.

Many devices can now be connected to the Internet. Smartphones can launch social media applications. New refrigerators have built-in cameras that consumers can access remotely. Modern cars come with

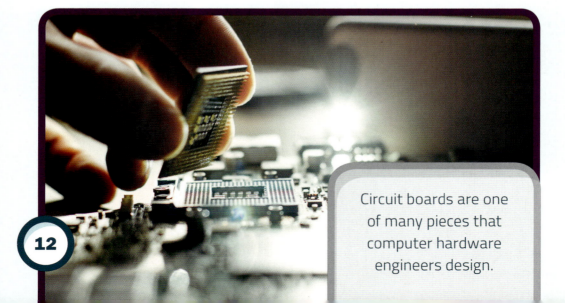

Circuit boards are one of many pieces that computer hardware engineers design.

computer navigation systems. All of these devices have computer parts designed by computer hardware engineers.

Most computer hardware engineers earn a bachelor's degree. These engineers also need to have good communication skills. They usually work as part of a team. Computer hardware engineers often work closely with software developers. The hardware engineers build computer parts that meet the developers' needs. For example, some applications need to use a lot of memory space. Good communication helps make sure computers work well.

16

Weight, in pounds (7.3 kg), of Apple's first portable computer from 1989.

- Computer hardware engineers design and build the parts that make up a computer.
- Many hardware engineers are focused on making computers smaller and lighter.
- Computer hardware engineers design computers for many different products, such as smartphones, refrigerators, and cars.
- Computer hardware engineers usually work in teams and need good communication skills.

The Macintosh Portable, Apple's first portable computer

Aerospace Engineers Take to the Skies

Aerospace engineers design and test everything that moves through air and space. For outer space, aerospace engineers design new rockets and satellites. They help keep the International Space Station running. These engineers design and test the satellites sent into Earth's orbit. Devices such as cell phones and GPS systems use these satellites every day.

Closer to Earth's surface, aerospace engineers design aircraft. They figure out how to make planes fly faster while carrying more people. The first commercial plane to fly across the Atlantic Ocean held 26 passengers. In comparison, the Airbus A380 jumbo jet has four floors and can carry 544 passengers. Aerospace engineers also have to make sure the aircraft they design can withstand changes in the weather.

Aerospace engineers design and test airplanes.

An illustration of what the Sputnik-1 satellite looked like in flight

Many aerospace engineers are focused on how to make aircraft quieter.

Some aerospace engineers work for NASA or the military. Others work for private companies. Whatever the field, aerospace engineers must be good at math. Many aerospace engineers take courses in physics in high school and college.

1957
Year when the Soviet Union launched the first satellite, called Sputnik.

- Aerospace engineers design things that move in outer space and through the air.
- Satellites are designed by aerospace engineers.
- Aerospace engineers try to figure out how to make aircraft fly faster and quieter.
- Aerospace engineers have to be good at math and physics.

DIGITAL GLOBE

Not all satellites are made by NASA or government agencies. A private company called Digital Globe has many satellites orbiting Earth. These satellites are equipped with cameras that take detailed pictures of Earth from above. Digital Globe sells some of these high-quality pictures to Google, Uber, and Facebook.

15

Forensic Engineers Figure Out Failures

In 2007, a bridge that was part of Interstate 35W in Minnesota collapsed into the Mississippi River. It happened during the evening rush hour. Many people were injured, and some died. To find out what went wrong, the state of Minnesota hired a team of forensic engineers.

Structures such as bridges, buildings, and tunnels sometimes fall apart or collapse. They do not work as they were supposed to. When that happens, governments and companies want to find out why. Forensic engineers typically start by inspecting the damage. They take pictures and gather samples. They look over the original plans civil engineers used to design the structures. Forensic engineers look for errors in design and construction.

The collapsed I-35W bridge

What they find helps to make future structures safer.

Like civil engineers, forensic engineers need to earn a bachelor's degree. Most also need to pass a state exam to practice engineering. Forensic engineers need to have good communication skills. They write reports about their findings. Sometimes they have to testify in court. Forensic engineers have to present their research in terms that nonexperts can understand.

58,495
Number of US bridges that were identified as structurally deficient in 2016.

- Sometimes structures such as bridges, buildings, and tunnels do not work the way they were supposed to.
- Forensic engineers investigate what went wrong.
- These engineers gather evidence and look over original plans to find errors.
- Forensic engineers need good communication skills to present their findings in written reports and while testifying in court.

Forensic engineers are often called in after hurricanes to find out if damages were caused by wind or by water.

Mechanical Engineers Keep Machines Running Smoothly

Mechanical engineers build all kinds of machines. Farm tractors, freezers, and wind turbines are all designed with the help of mechanical engineers. Mechanical engineers can choose from a wide range of jobs. They work in nearly every field.

For example, American Ron Toomer earned his degree in mechanical engineering in 1961. After graduating, he helped design satellites. Then he worked for NASA to engineer a heat shield to protect the Apollo shuttle during its return to Earth. But his true passion was designing roller coasters. Over 30 years, Toomer designed more than 80 roller coasters throughout the world. Other mechanical engineers helped design each part of the coasters. They made the cars, the motors, the tracks, and the brakes.

Ron Toomer's Corkscrew roller coaster at Cedar Point in Sandusky, Ohio, remains popular today.

Mechanical engineering technicians work alongside mechanical engineers. They perform many of the same tasks. Technicians help with planning and testing. They draw plans for engineers to review. Technicians usually need to earn an associate's degree. Mechanical engineers need to have a bachelor's degree.

14
Percentage of US engineers who are women.

- Mechanical engineers work in a variety of fields and jobs.
- Many mechanical engineers design and work on things that move.
- Roller coasters cannot be built without the help of mechanical engineers.
- Engineers often work closely with mechanical engineering technicians.

RUBE GOLDBERG

Rube Goldberg was a cartoonist. He was also an engineer. He drew cartoons of complicated machines. His machines connected many everyday items to perform simple jobs. One machine was called No More Oversleeping. It used a paper bag, water, a ball, a rope, and a ladle. Goldberg's drawings became very famous. His name now means a very complicated invention that does a very simple task.

Environmental Engineers Protect the Planet

Environmental engineers work to keep the planet as healthy as possible. Everything that humans build has an effect on the environment. Some environmental engineers study those effects. They examine how natural resources, such as soil and water, have changed over time. Other engineers work to reduce environmental problems that have already happened. They find new ways to recycle materials. They search for ways to reduce air pollution.

Federal and local governments employ a number of environmental engineers. These engineers help develop environmental policies. They make recommendations about where and how buildings can be constructed. They help cities understand how their water use impacts the local environment.

Governments and companies also hire environmental engineers to help during disasters. For example, environmental engineers visit oil spills. They help figure out how best to

The Deepwater Horizon oil spill in the Gulf of Mexico in 2010 was the largest marine oil spill in US history.

remove oil from the water. They can determine when the water is safe again. These engineers also make recommendations for how to avoid future disasters.

Some engineers get their bachelor's degree in environmental engineering. Others earn a general engineering degree. Besides taking many math and science courses, environmental engineers need to have good problem-solving skills. It is hard for many people to change their habits. Engineers have to look for environmentally friendly ways to produce the same results as older technologies that people are familiar with using.

55,100
Number of US environmental engineers working in 2014.

- Environmental engineers help protect the planet's natural resources.
- Federal and local governments work with environmental engineers to develop environmental policies.
- Engineers help clean up environmental disasters and figure out how to avoid future ones.
- Environmental engineers need to have good problem-solving skills to make functional yet environmentally friendly designs.

Environmental engineers examine water samples in flooded areas.

Marine Engineers Explore New Depths

Almost three-fourths of our planet is covered with ocean. Yet most of our oceans have never been explored. That is because exploring in deep water is difficult. At 13,000 feet (3,962 m) underwater, the temperature is close to freezing. There is no sunlight. And the pressure is intense. People could not survive down there.

Some marine engineers create equipment to explore where humans cannot go. Engineers can design underwater robots called autonomous underwater vehicles (AUVs). Some AUVs can dive three to four miles (4.8 to 6.4 km) under water. The AUVs can map the ocean floor. They can take soil samples, measure deep-sea temperatures, and monitor pollution levels.

Most marine engineers develop vehicles that stay near the surface of the water. They make sure aircraft carriers and sailboats work properly. They test designs for submarines.

Many marine engineers work in offices, but others go out and test or inspect the ships they design.

Wind turbines at sea

Engineers figure out ways to make them even quieter. Some marine engineers also design oil rigs for offshore drilling. They may also develop tools that help scientists.

The work marine engineers do often includes many types of engineering. They use mechanical engineering when designing a system to make ships move. They use electrical engineering when thinking about power onboard ships.

12

Percentage of marine engineers who work for the federal government.

- Some marine engineers build underwater robots to explore the deep sea.
- Most marine engineers work with vehicles that operate near the surface of the water.
- Marine engineers have to use many types of engineering.

THINK ABOUT IT

Some marine engineers design wind farms that are stationed in the ocean. Wind farms are a source of renewable energy, but they could hurt ocean life. Does the need to reduce the use of fossil fuels outweigh the need to protect the environment in the sea?

Electrical Engineers Develop New Ways to Use Power

Look at any device that uses electricity. Chances are it was designed by an electrical engineer. Electrical engineers study electronic parts. Some examples of these parts include resistors and capacitors. Electrical engineers study and figure out ways to put these parts together.

Electrical engineers study current and voltage. Current is the flow of electricity. Voltage is the intensity of that current.

Electrical engineers work in many industries. Some work for manufacturing companies. They design electrical systems in cars, ships, and planes. They may design electronic equipment for communication devices.

Electrical engineers can also work for power companies. They design control systems to make sure electricity is delivered to homes safely. They make repairs when the electricity goes out. These electrical

Electrical engineers inspect equipment to make sure it meets safety standards.

engineers need to be prepared to work nights and weekends. Outages can happen at any time.

Electrical engineers need to earn a bachelor's degree in engineering. They have to be good at math. Electrical engineers should also be comfortable working with other engineers. They often work as a team with mechanical engineers and software engineers.

450,000
Number of miles (724,205 km) of high-voltage power lines in the United States.

- Electrical engineers study how electricity works.
- Electrical engineers work in many industries, including manufacturing.
- Other electrical engineers work for power companies.
- Electrical engineers need to be good at math and comfortable working on a team with other engineers.

Power lines lead from the power plant to the consumer.

Chemical Engineers Search for the Right Formulas

All fields of engineering use math and science. But some engineers heavily rely on the branch of science called chemistry. Chemical engineers study how different chemicals interact to make products and manufacturing better.

Some chemical engineers spend their entire careers examining one element: oxygen. When oxygen reacts with other chemicals, this process is called oxidation. Oxidation causes rust on metals. It makes food turn brown. Chemical engineers

Many chemical engineers work in labs.

Chemical engineers research ways to improve products or manufacturing.

study the process of oxidation and think of ways to slow it down.

$97,360

Average salary for chemical engineers in the United States in 2015.

- Chemical engineers use chemistry more than other fields of engineering.
- Some chemical engineers specialize in studying oxygen.
- Food companies hire chemical engineers to reverse engineer the taste of certain foods.
- Future chemical engineers should apply for internships to gain professional experience.

Some chemical engineers use reverse engineering. For example, food companies often want to produce products that taste like cheese. However, cheese is perishable. It spoils quickly. Food companies hire chemical engineers to find a substitute. Engineers begin by examining what cheese is made out of. They look at the chemicals present in cheese. Then they mix different substances to mimic the taste.

Chemical engineers need to earn a bachelor's degree in chemical engineering. Future engineers should take as many science classes as possible in high school. Internships while in college are a good way to gain professional experience.

Other Jobs to Consider

Broadcast Engineer

Description: Set up and operate video and audio equipment for radio and television stations
Training/Education: No formal education needed
Outlook: Steady
Average salary: $41,780

Industrial Engineering Technician

Description: Help organize people and equipment to make large-scale systems run smoothly and safely
Training/Education: Associate's degree
Outlook: In decline
Average salary: $53,780

Health and Safety Engineer

Description: Develop procedures and systems to keep people from getting hurt
Training/Education: Bachelor's degree
Outlook: Steady
Average salary: $84,600

Materials Engineer

Description: Develop and study materials to make better products
Training/Education: Bachelor's degree
Outlook: Steady
Average salary: $91,110

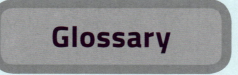

Glossary

application
A program that allows a computer to perform certain tasks.

biomedical
Relating to both biology and medicine.

capacitors
Devices that store electrical energy.

employ
To hire.

equipped
Made ready or prepared.

inspect
To look at closely.

licensed
To be formally given permission to do something.

mimic
To imitate.

physics
The science that deals with facts about matter, energy, and motion.

resistors
Devices used to control the flow of electricity.

satellites
Human-made objects orbiting the earth.

technicians
People who are specialists in certain jobs.

For More Information

Books

Cunningham, Kevin. *Roller Coasters: From Concept to Consumer.* New York: Children's Press, 2013.

Rusch, Elizabeth. *Electrical Wizard: How Nikola Tesla Lit Up the World.* Somerville, MA: Candlewick Press, 2013.

Smibert, Angie. *Environmental Engineering in the Real World.* Minneapolis, MN: Abdo Publishing, 2017.

Visit 12StoryLibrary.com

Scan the code or use your school's login at **12StoryLibrary.com** for recent updates about this topic and a full digital version of this book. Enjoy free access to:

- Digital ebook
- Breaking news updates
- Live content feeds
- Videos, interactive maps, and graphics
- Additional web resources

Note to educators: Visit 12StoryLibrary.com/register to sign up for free premium website access. Enjoy live content plus a full digital version of every 12-Story Library book you own for every student at your school.

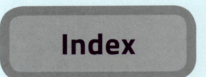

Index

aerospace engineers, 14–15
associate's degree, 9, 19
autonomous underwater vehicles, 22

bachelor's degree, 7, 9, 11, 13, 17, 19, 21, 25, 27
biomedical engineers, 6–7

chemical engineers, 4, 26–27
civil engineers, 4, 8–9, 16–17
computers, 11, 12–13
construction, 8–9, 16
Curiosity, 11

electrical engineers, 24–25
environmental engineers, 20–21

forensic engineers, 16–17

Goldberg, Rube, 19

Hoover Dam, 4, 8

International Space Station, 14
internship, 7, 27

makerspaces, 5
manufacturing, 24, 26
marine engineers, 22–23
mechanical engineers, 18–19, 25

NASA, 10–11, 15, 18
natural resources, 20

Opportunity, 11

physics, 15
pollution, 20, 22
prosthetics, 6

robotics engineers, 10–11
robots, 10–11, 22
roller coasters, 18
rover, 4, 10–11

satellites, 14, 15, 18
solar panels, 4

Toomer, Ron, 18

About the Author

Vicki C. Hayes spent seven years as a broadcast engineer for ABC Radio News and WNET, the PBS television station in New York. She is currently a teacher and writer.